The Practical Harmonist
at the Harpsichord

Da Capo Press Music Reprint Series

MUSIC EDITOR
BEA FRIEDLAND
Ph.D., City University of New York

The Practical Harmonist
at the Harpsichord

by

FRANCESCO GASPARINI

translated by

FRANK S. STILLINGS

edited by

DAVID L. BURROWS

Da Capo Press · New York · 1980

Library of Congress Cataloging in Publication Data

Gasparini, Francesco, 1668-1727.
   The practical harmonist at the harpsichord.

   (Da Capo Press music reprint series)
   Translation of L'armonico pratico al cimbalo.
   Reprint of the 1968 ed. published by Yale University
Press, New Haven, which was issued as #1 of Music
theory in translation series.
   1. Thorough bass. 2. Musical accompaniment.
I. Burrows, David L. II. Title. III. Series:
Music theory translation series; 1.
[MT49.G3513 1980]   781.3'2   79-26854
ISBN 0-306-76017-7

Published by Da Capo Press, Inc.
A Subsidiary of Plenum Publishing Corporation
227 West 17th Street, New York, N.Y. 10011

MUSIC THEORY TRANSLATION SERIES, 1

Claude V. Palisca, *Editor*

The Practical Harmonist
at the Harpsichord

by FRANCESCO GASPARINI

translated by
FRANK S. STILLINGS

edited by
DAVID L. BURROWS

YALE UNIVERSITY PRESS, NEW HAVEN AND LONDON

Foreword

A TRANSLATION OF GASPARINI'S TREATISE ON FIGURED bass scarcely needs justification during the present revival of interest in baroque music. The pivotal role of the harpsichordist in the proper rendition of this music has created an urgent need for formal instruction in realizing a *basso continuo*—and especially for realizing it in an authentic, appropriate fashion. Despite the best efforts of editors of baroque music to provide ready-made realizations, it is increasingly clear that the only solution acceptable to all is the original one, in which a properly trained keyboard player provides his own realization tailored for the occasion.

Aside from this purely practical purpose of a figured bass treatise, there is a wider purpose that touches on the education of every musician, amateur or professional. Figured bass, long identical with the teaching of harmony, can lead us to an understanding of the very fabric of our traditional music. Just as we now realize that placing chords over a bass was the first step in the development of modern harmonic practice, so we also realize that learning to play on a bass in the traditional manner is the first step in the mastery of that practice. The student can begin his study of harmony in no better way than with figured bass.

There is no better introduction to figured bass than Gasparini's *L'Armonico Pratico al Cimbalo* of 1708. Born in 1668, Gasparini studied in Rome under Bernardo Pasquini, was then professionally occupied in Venice, and later Rome, until his death in 1727; thus he worked amid the operas and cantatas of Pasquini, Bononcini, and Alessandro Scarlatti. Writing in Venice shortly after 1700, Gasparini stood at the historical time and place best suited to a clear understanding of Italian baroque music—and therefore of figured bass harmony. Late enough to include a comprehensive treatment of mature baroque style, early enough to avoid the sometimes intricate, sometimes extravagant procedures of the mid-eighteenth century, Gasparini's formulation was, indeed, the classic one, providing the core of later, more elaborate systems such as Heinichen's. In summarizing what was essential in seventeenth-century practice, Gasparini presented the basic facts of traditional harmony in a simple, elegant way.

Gasparini's treatise begins at the beginning, showing the student how to place his hands on the keyboard to produce harmony. From there the work proceeds through ascending, then descending motion by step and by leap, always providing a basic rule along with enough variants and exceptions to reflect actual harmonic practice and to furnish musical interest. All that is essential, but no more, is included; indeed, one might criticize, from a theoretical point of view, some of the rough-and-ready solutions to basic problems, for instance parallel fifths and octaves. But Gasparini is writing for the player, not the composer: his rules cover those aspects of style that a player, accompanying from a bass—perhaps even at sight—can be expected to control, not necessarily those niceties that a composer, working at leisure, must attain. For this reason too, Gasparini's treatise is well-suited to the needs of the beginning student, who cannot be expected to grasp the reasons for provisions against sins he cannot yet hear. As a reward for the student who perseveres through the treatment of triads and chords of the sixth, Gasparini provides toward the end a rich dessert of sevenths and ninths—not to speak of those magnificent diminished sevenths and acciaccaturas, requiring as many notes as the hands can put down "for fuller sonority," upon which the author's fame has depended in our own time.

*   *   *

The problems of translation have been treated too often and too well to be rehearsed here; enough to say that we have not hesitated to be as literal, or as free, as the original text and clear English allowed and required. Gasparini's meaning is almost always apparent; his language presents the English translator with few real problems. Modern English equivalents, drawn from the standard vocabulary of the subject, have been found for most technical terms. For the few exceptions, the meaning and justification will usually be self-evident. Still, it may be helpful to comment here on a few matters.

The most interesting problem of terminology occurs in Chapter VIII, devoted to keys and modulations. Throughout this chapter Gasparini was struggling to express concepts for which a standard vocabulary did not yet exist; he hesitated between old terms and concepts no longer relevant, and new, pragmatic ones. Here we have let stand his occasionally awkward expressions, since these are of great interest to the history of theory. In this chapter the term "Tono," always capitalized, is used to designate a higher tonal order—and always has this meaning when capitalized (except in one instance where the typesetter, understandably confused, set "mezzo Tono"); but the meaning of "Tono" changes in the course of the chapter from "mode" to "key." We have translated the term now one way, now the other, according to its meaning, and have marked with a footnote what seemed to be the principal transition from one meaning to the other. The reader can obtain the original appearance by reading both "mode" and "key" as "tone," noting at the same time the transitional use of this term.

In Chapter IX we have retained Gasparini's term "mordent"—at the risk of momentary confusion—because there seemed to be no alternative. The original term "acciaccatura" has, of course, been retained. In Chapter VII we have followed Gasparini in referring to diminished sevenths as "minor," since this happens only a few times; we have, however, placed this "minor" in quotation marks.

Gasparini sometimes provides pitch-letters with solmization syllables, for example G *sol re ut*. These have been preserved, on the grounds that it will do the student no harm to be familiar with them; in any case they offer no cause for confusion or obscurity, being easily passed over. Inconsistently perhaps, we have rendered "b.molle," "b.quadro," and "diesis" always as "flat," "natural," and "sharp"; but here the original meaning is not immediately apparent to the modern reader, nor is Gasparini's own usage (he sometimes uses merely the sign) so consistent. In the musical examples—except in Chapter III—we have substituted a natural for a flat when the latter canceled a sharp, in accordance with modern practice.

The word "andante" has been variously translated. It is, of course, a household word in Italian, and has been so interpreted in Ex.136 ("Common cadence" for "Cadenze andanti"), the more technical meanings not seeming applicable in that case. But even its technical meanings pose problems, for in cases like Ex.138, the expression "più andante" certainly means "faster." There is, incidentally, other evidence for such a reading; one can make out a good case for understanding "andante" as "going right along" in its seventeenth-century meaning.

In accordance with seventeenth-century practice, Gasparini beats "one-to-the-bar": each measure of common time receives one beat ("battuta"), a downbeat at the beginning of the measure and an upbeat halfway through. A "mezza battuta," therefore, is a half-measure, and has been translated as such, but it is of great importance for an understanding of Gasparini's harmonic rhythm to be aware of his own notion of beat. In triple time the beat also falls on the measure; here the downbeat is traditionally twice as long as the upbeat, hence notes that begin on the second beat and extend through the third may be regarded as syncopated.

On two occasions Gasparini speaks of "tempo perfetto" ("perfect time"), but means thereby common time. In the first case (at Ex.31), which deals with quarter-note motion, Gasparini's words "in tempo perfetto, o binario" could mean "in perfect (triple) time, or in duple time," or "in perfect, that is, duple time"; the quarter-note progressions he describes, however, would be too complex for the fast pace of $\frac{3}{1}$, the only triple time that could be involved. The second case (at Ex.62) allows only the second interpretation, in which "tempo perfetto" is taken as another name for duple, or common time. In any case, the triple measures of the seventeenth century are—properly speaking—not in "perfect time" (this not having been in common use since the early sixteenth century), but are proportions, as Gasparini elsewhere calls them. Gasparini's term "tempo," when it means the time-unit equal to a quarter-note, has been translated as "count," hence "for two counts." The traditional names for the various rhythmic values have been given their modern equivalents, as "half-note" for "minima."

The rendering of the musical examples has required more adjustment than the text itself, in order that no peculiarity of notation might distract the student, while at the same time retaining as much as possible the form of the original. No reduction of times-values was made, even for the few examples in $\frac{3}{1}$ or $\frac{3}{2}$; these, of course, go much faster than their appearance suggests, but that in any case is clear from Gasparini's remarks. The soprano clef has been replaced by the "violin" clef, the tenor clef by the bass clef; but exception has been made, particularly in the first examples, where the original clefs seemed more appropriate. The familiar cursive (oval) note-forms have been substituted for the rhomboidal ones formerly used for typeset; accordingly, eighth- and sixteenth-notes have been beamed in appropriate groupings, except in a few cases illustrating recitative.

Barlines presented the greatest problem: Gasparini used the single bar to mark off separate instances of the progression in question; but the single bar is also used in those examples that have, or imply, a time signature, hence a regular measure. Apparently put off by this ambiguity, the original editor did not escape inconsistency; nor have the present ones. We have used the double bar, rather than the single one, to mark off successive instances of the same example. These instances may, or may not, be playable consecutively; but they need not be so played for the sake of the example. When a time-signature (C) is present in the original (or, being implied, has been added), then the single bar has been used regularly in accordance with modern practice.

Gasparini places his figures sometimes above, sometimes below the bass; sometimes the greater figures are above the lesser ones, sometimes not. It is perhaps more convenient to put the figures above the bass, but we have put them below, with the greater above the lesser, that being the more common practice nowadays. In a few cases an essential figure, obviously missing or wrong, has been supplied in parentheses; no attempt has been made, however, to "complete" the figuring, for this not only leads to ridiculous extremes, but is contrary to the original intent, which is to teach the student to play from an *un*figured bass, deriving the nature of the chord from the nature of the progression. Omission of figures, then, speeds the student's progress, while unnecessary addition hinders it.

To all of this there is one notable group of exceptions. Gasparini occasionally writes out a progression in "tablature," a form of keyboard score. After much hesitation, the editors decided to leave these examples as they stood, partly for lack of a modern equivalent that retained certain important features of the original, partly because the original, in its external appearance, bears a striking resemblance to those difficult "unmeasured preludes" found in French keyboard music of the later seventeenth century—for which Gasparini's examples in tablature might conceivably prove helpful. Also left untouched (except, as always, in the manner of forming the notes themselves) are certain examples showing the constitution of intervals, especially diminished fifths and sevenths; here the original notation seemed as good as any. And in Ex.83 the ties, showing where to sustain a note in the upper part over movement in the bass, are Gasparini's makeshift for a later notation.

Gasparini, or his editor, consistently places each musical example at the point where it is needed, directly following the discussion that concerns it. We have endeavored to do the same; only in two or three trivial cases have several examples been placed on one line, for purely typographical reasons. Similarly, the format of the last chapter has been changed considerably, without, however, changing the substance. The incomplete state of Ex. 141 was probably caused by the requirements of the original format; the student can easily fill in the missing notes himself.

Eitner's *Quellen-Lexikon* lists five editions by the original Venetian publisher Bortoli—the first in 1708, a second in 1715, a third in 1729, a fourth in 1745 (there is at Yale what seems to be a reprint of this fourth edition, dated MDCCLIV), and a fifth in 1764; other editions by Silvani in Bologna in 1713 and 1722; finally a sixth, revised edition by Seb. Valle in Venice in 1802. Our translation has been made from the first edition, whose title page is reproduced on page 2. Few emendations have been necessary; they are indicated in the footnotes. The later editions are mentioned only in a very few cases where they provide better readings, their numerous minor differences not being noted here. Except for portions in F. T. Arnold's *The Art of Accompaniment from a Thorough-Bass* (London, 1931), Gasparini's treatise has not previously been published in English translation.

RICHARD L. CROCKER

Yale University
January 1963

Acknowledgments

THE EDITORS OF THE *Journal of Music Theory* WISH TO express their appreciation to Brooks Shepard Jr., for reading the manuscript; Marion Gushee, for copying the musical examples; Adrienne Suddard, for readying the manuscript; and the Library of Congress, for furnishing a photograph of the original title page.

Contents

Contents

*The Practical Harmonist
at the Harpsichord*

L'ARMONICO
PRATICO
AL CIMBALO.

Regole, Offervazioni, ed Avvertimenti per ben
fuonare il Baffo, e accompagnare fopra il
Cimbalo, Spinetta, ed Organo

DI

FRANCESCO GASPARINI
LUCCHESE.

*Maeftro di Coro del Pio Ofpedale della Pietà in
Venezia, ed Accademico Filarmonico*

DEDICATO

All' Illuftriffimo, ed Eccellentiffimo Signor

GIROLAMO ASCANIO
GIUSTINIANI
Nobile Veneto.

✽✽✽ ✽✽✽

IN VENEZIA, MDCCVIII.
Appreffo Antonio Bortoli.
CON LICENZA DE' SUPERIORI, E PRIVILEGIO.

The Practical Harmonist
at the Harpsichord

Rules, Observations, and Admonitions
for Realizing the Bass
and Accompanying on the Harpsichord, Spinet, and Organ

by FRANCESCO GASPARINI
of Lucca

Choirmaster at the *Pio Ospedale della Pietà* in Venice
and a Member of the *Accademia Filarmonica*

DEDICATED TO
The Most Illustrious and Worthy
GIROLAMO ASCANIO GIUSTINIANI
Noble Venetian

VENICE, 1708
At Antonio Bortoli's

BY PRIVILEGE, AND WITH PERMISSION OF THE AUTHORITIES

Most Illustrious and Excellent Sir:

IF A LARGE SEA DOES NOT REFUSE THE MEAGER TRIBUTES of a small stream, gently receiving it into its vast bosom, then can I, with assurance, offer, as unto a sea of matchless gentleness, this tribute of my feeble intellect (insignificant though it is) to the greatness of your Excellency, who benignly receives every gesture of reverence from the least of his servants. I, who from your first years recognized in your most noble countenance the true image of virtue, am not now misled as I dedicate to you this small labor of mine, in the hope that it will be accepted by you with that generosity one already admires in the lofty, though youthful, thoughts of a childhood wherein the spirit looms so great, of a youth wherein a wisdom more than mature can be discerned. And if, among so many books on harmony already brought into the light of the world, the one that I present to you seems the least significant—like a chattering bird that, having only voice and feathers, in competition with winged flocks lacks the strength to raise itself to the level of the others—nonetheless I do not fear its defeat in the test of flight. Mounting the wings of the Giustinian eagle,[1] it will be able to boast of a triumphant victory over all rivals at the end of its journey. Any glory I might have deserved for having composed this book, crude and poorly made as it is, derives from the presence at its very opening of the esteemed name of Your Excellency. It would be sufficient for me if a benign glance at some of these pages were to be granted by you, whose most excellent taste is so favorably inclined to the diversion of music. If these please you, I should hope that, through them, the harpsichord will partake of that honor enjoyed by those other musical instruments so sweetly sounded by the gentle hand of Your Excellency. And in truth, music has been known so nobly

---

[1] Girolamo Ascanio Giustiniani (1697–1749) came from a Venetian family long known for their support of the arts. His most notable contribution was the poetry for Benedetto Marcello's *Estro poetico-armonico* (Venice, Lovisa, 1724–26).

to satisfy you that it may well hope to find in your patronage its long-desired refuge. Let it be said, to the greater glory of Your Excellency, that the practice of music has not in the least prejudiced those studies to which you must apply yourself at your present tender age in order to prove yourself the worthy son of a father, and descendant of a grandfather, who, together, are the compendium of science, the splendor of their country, and two luminaries of the Adriatic skies. And so this little offspring of mine beseeches your all-powerful protection; like a fledgling pilgrim setting out to make himself known to the world, it will fear neither tempests, nor shocks of boulders, nor reverses of fortune, as long as it is guided by the rays of that splendor it will receive from the guardian spirit of such esteemed patronage. May Your Excellency then condescend to accept this testimony of my devotion, because of the burning desire I have of being considered—as, with most profound reverence, I undersign myself—

Your Excellency's most humble, most devoted,
and most obsequious servant,

FRANCESCO GASPARINI

To the Reader

YOU WILL BE SURPRISED AT SEEING A WORK YOU NEVER expected brought into the light of the world. First, because you did not consider me an organist and, consequently, as being well-suited to treat such material. In the second place, I know that you will say, "Why waste time on so useless and unnecessary a labor? There is not a journeyman teacher who does not know how to impart it in a few lessons, nor a beginning student who does not understand it within a few months." I reply that experience has not proven to me the validity of your opinions. And if you will condescend to glance quickly with tolerant eyes through these pages, you will perhaps find something new in them that will not displease you. If I write plainly and without the niceties of a cultivated style—so be it; I shall not be hurt if you consider me a musician, not a rhetorician. For if you are then determined to make me the target of your criticism, it will confirm me a little in my role of virtuoso, of whom it would be proper to make such a target; thus you will honor me more than offend me. If, on the other hand, you are so agreeable of mind and so gentle of spirit that it pleases you to bear with me, then I ask, in presenting this work to you, that you receive it as a friend and that you regard me as desirous of helping my fellow man in having—as a good Catholic—published it and written it all by myself. All good go with you.

To Organ Teachers

Forgive me, beloved colleagues, if from some feeble intent of this work it should seem to you, at first glance, that I have aspired to intrude upon your knowledge and interests by tempting anyone to approach the task of learning this art without your assistance. But if you will reconsider, you will perceive that my intent benefits you. That wise physician who publishes secrets and remedies for the well-being of mankind does not do it to hurt his colleagues and successors in the art, but to help his neighbor. Thus, my real goal has been to assist the student, to ease the labor of the beginner, to encourage and entice the amateur, and to lessen the work of the teacher. Bear with me, harbor no ill feelings, and may God be with you.

Introduction

YOU WILL NOT DENY (WHETHER YOU ARE A PROFESSIONAL or amateur of music) that to master this noble and beautiful art requires principally three things, namely, resolve, application, and a good teacher. But even though it is asserted by some weighty authorities that these three suffice to make a perfect musician, I agree only in principle. In practice I differ, for it is not enough to say, "I have decided, am determined, and really want to learn music; I will apply myself to it as much as I am able; and I have a first-rate, diligent teacher." All this is considerable, in fact indispensable, but if a certain natural disposition does not accompany it, the greater part of what is necessary for arriving at the sound practice of correct, well-modulated harmony will be missing.

Of all these things the easiest—and the most difficult—is this natural disposition: easiest, since it is a gift uniquely from God and nature; most difficult, or I might rather say impossible, because at no price is it ever acquired. Resolve is derived easily from one's own disposition. Application is the most arduous, since few like to work. A good teacher is the thing most rare, because not all good teachers instruct willingly, not all communicate easily, not all students of music can afford good teachers, nor can these be found everywhere (although today, to be sure, there are more teachers than students). In the meantime, seeing many eager to learn to accompany, or realize the bass on the harpsichord, organ, or perhaps another keyboard instrument, I hope with this little volume of mine to

9

convey the spirit of accompanying, lessening the labor of practice, and facilitating the task with many observations useful not only to students, but also to those teachers who will not scorn my advice.

It is certainly true that in order to become a truly skilled organist, one must make a special study of scores, particularly of the toccatas, fugues, ricercars, etc. of Frescobaldi or of other excellent composers, and to study under able, learned teachers. Finally, accompaniment demands not only a grasp of all the valid rules of counterpoint, but also good taste, natural-ness, and a ready recognition of the style of a composition, in order to play in ensembles as well as to accompany the singer with flexibility and discretion, encouraging, satisfying, and supporting rather than confusing him. But among the many who have the ability to learn, I note that the greater part, as I said, do not like to work, some because they do not have the will to apply themselves continually, as the preparation of a score requires, some because they do not have time, and some because they are advanced in age. It is indeed a study for youths, who, whether through inclination, or fear of the lash, or emulation, but mainly through the pene-tration of their intellects, learn so easily that they do themselves great credit. There are an infinite number of nobles, gentlemen, ladies, and princes, who feel an inclination toward music, but should they start in, it is certain that, because of their customary preoccupation with studies of literature or other gentlemanly exercises, a generation, so to speak, would not suffice them to arrive at the playing of four notes. (Of course, I do not state this as an absolute rule, because some of them are of such high spirit and ready wit that they absorb admirably everything to which they apply themselves.) So, too, there are those singers who desire either a greater knowledge and grasp of singing, or would like to be able to ac-company themselves on occasion, but who cannot or do not wish to de-vote much time to study, since work is sometimes harmful to the voice.

I conclude, finally, that whoever can apply himself to such study will do very well and will derive from my work some benefit for accompany-ing or realizing the bass. For those who wish to begin learning accom-paniment without other studies in scoring or counterpoint, I have tried to explain things simply, starting from the naming of the notes, the method of forming consonances, the movements of the hands, etc. Having discovered from countless observations of my own that many rules given by others in times past, correct though they may be, meet with endless exceptions because of the great variations, the motifs, inspirations, caprices, modulations, and movements of the bass used especially today by our modern composers—nevertheless I have resolved to put forward from the beginning those same rules, since I do not wish to boast of bringing the student to perfection, but rather hope to be of such assistance that my labor may not be judged useless and vain by him who may be willing and able to profit from it.

CHAPTER I

The Names and Positions of the Notes

THE STUDENT SHOULD MEMORIZE THE NAMES OF THE notes and their positions in all the clefs. This can be conveniently practiced by using the table placed in the last chapter of this book.

Ex.1 *The clefs*

C sol fa ut   F fa ut   G sol re ut

Here are the names of the notes:

A *la mi re*
B *fa,* B *mi*
C *sol fa ut*
D *la sol re*
E *la mi*
F *fa ut*
G *sol re ut*

The teacher should then explain, with the help of the following example, the five registers, namely, grave, acute, superacute, most acute, and most grave.

Ex.2

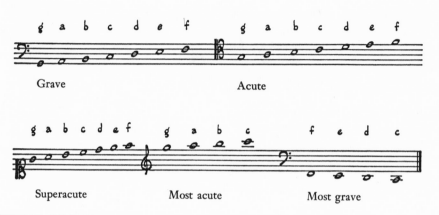

Grave   Acute

Superacute   Most acute   Most grave

Another example, showing the location of all the natural keys:

Ex.3

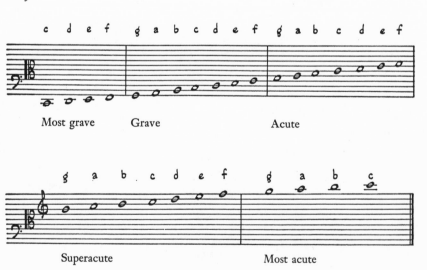

Most grave   Grave   Acute

Superacute   Most acute

Next comes the practical recognition of all the keys. In order to facilitate this, observe first the disposition of the natural, or white keys, which are said to be of the diatonic genus, and then observe the accidentals, which are the black keys, said to be of the chromatic genus. Observe that these black keys are grouped in threes and twos, between which are two white keys not separated by a black one. Thus the names of the keys can be quickly and easily learned by remembering their location, since in among the three black keys are G *sol re ut* and A *la mi re*. Between the other two black keys is D *la sol re*. It is the same in all registers of the keyboard, except that on some harpsichords some contrabass strings are added below the lowest octave.

The black keys, which are of the chromatic genus, are indicated by the major or minor accidentals, the sharp and the flat,[2] using now this one, now that—as will become clear in the course of these rules.

Next learn the positions of the notes in the clef of F *fa ut* on the fourth line, that is, the bass clef, as shown below.

Ex.4

In order to place the hands on the keys to produce a correct and perfect harmony, it is necessary to know the musical intervals. These are the second, third, fourth, fifth, sixth, seventh, octave, ninth, and tenth. One may continue up to the twenty-second and beyond, but for greater clarity every interval larger than an octave is considered doubled. Hence the tenth is called a third, the eleventh a fourth, the twelfth a fifth, these having the same relationship; these doubled intervals are called compound or decompound.[3] For example, the fifteenth is called the compound octave, and the octave above, that is, the twenty-second, is called the de-

---

[2] "Diesis ♯ e b.molle ♭." See the Foreword.

[3] Gasparini wrote "composti, o decomposti."

compound, or doubly compound octave. In the same way the tenth may be called the compound third, the twelfth the compound fifth.

Ex.5 *The intervals*

From these it will be easy to work out all the others at the keyboard.

Of these numbers, or intervals, the third, fifth, sixth, and octave are called consonances. All the others, that is to say the second, fourth, seventh, and ninth, are called dissonances. Of the four consonances, two are perfect and two imperfect. The perfect consonances are the fifth and octave. The imperfect consonances are the third and sixth; they are called imperfect because they are subject to the major and minor accidentals—as will become clear further on.

CHAPTER II

How to Form Harmony with the Consonances

IN ORDER TO ACCOMPANY EVERY NOTE AND PROVIDE IT WITH perfect harmony, it is necessary to add to it the third, fifth, and octave. This serves as a general and infallible rule, unless it is clear that the note requires either a sixth or some other accompaniment of a passing dissonance, as will be seen later on. The third is natural if it is formed by the natural keys. Using these, one should practice carefully, beginning as follows.

Ex.6   Ex.7   Ex.8   Ex.9

In order to harmonize the first note G *sol re ut*, one spreads out the left hand, placing the little finger on G-grave, which is the fundamental note; next the index finger on D, which will be the fifth; then the thumb on G-acute, which will be the octave. The right hand follows with the index finger on D-acute, which will be another fifth; then the ring finger on the G following, which will be another octave; and finally the little finger on the B-superacute which follows. This is the third, or tenth, and with it the harmony of the fundamental note G *sol re ut* is complete. In moving from one note to another one must disturb the right hand as little as possible; as the bass changes one should see whether one note of the accompaniment can remain fixed, the others moving only stepwise, either up or down.

Proceeding then to C *sol fa ut* (Ex.7) move the left hand up a fourth, placing it on C with its octave. Place the index finger of the right hand on E-acute, which will be the third; the middle finger on the following G, which will be the fifth; then the little finger on the higher C-superacute, which will be the octave. Proceeding to A *la mi re* (Ex.8), move the left hand down a third to A-grave, E its fifth, and A its octave. Move the right hand in the manner indicated above for G, to the keys one step higher, which will be E, A, and C. D *la sol re* (Ex.9) follows, harmonized in the way noted above for C *sol fa ut*, using the keys one step higher, which will be D, A, and D in the left hand, and F, A, and D in the right. Those who understand a little about tablature will find all these notes in the following example.

Ex.10

For the present we will not consider those octaves or fifths that are prohibited, that is, two octaves or two fifths that follow one another in parallel motion; later on I will show how to avoid or correct such errors. Nor need thought be given to the doubling of the consonances, although this is a good thing. When the player is skilled he must endeavor to employ as many notes as possible in order to bring out greater harmony.

Let the beginning student take care to learn thoroughly and confidently the four above-named notes, together with their consonances, always counting up from the fundamental note. Be sure to place the hands carefully so that each finger assumes a natural position, not forced or twisted, or too straight, but poised on the keys, relaxed, supple, and with appropriate readiness.

After this, harmonize the following notes.

Ex.11   Ex.12   Ex.13   Ex.14

C *sol fa ut* is harmonized as described above. For F *fa ut* place the ring finger of the left hand on F, which is the fundamental note; then the index finger on A, which will be the third; and the thumb on C, which will be the fifth. The right hand follows with the index finger on F, which will be the octave; the ring finger on A, which will be another third; and the little finger on C, which will be another fifth. This is called for convenience the position of the fifth, because the left hand alone forms a fifth, just as when the left hand forms an octave it is called the position of the octave.

D *la sol re* follows, and can be harmonized in the manner given above. Afterwards, G *sol re ut* acute (Ex.12) will be harmonized in the position of the fifth, just as was F *fa ut*, moving the hand one step higher, that is, with G,B,D in the left hand and with G,B,D of the superacute octave in the right. E *la mi* (Ex.13) follows in the position of the octave like D *la sol re*, but one step higher, that is, with E,B,E in the left hand and G,B,E in the right. The last note, A *la mi re* (Ex.14) follows, and the left hand may be placed so as to form a third, that is, with the ring finger on A and the index finger on C, which will be its third. Place the right hand with the index finger on E, which will be the fifth; the ring finger on A, which will be the octave; and the little finger on C, which will be the tenth, or another third. This A *la mi re* may also be realized in the position of the fifth, like the G *sol re ut* acute, that is, with A,C,E in the left hand and A,C,E of the superacute octave in the right.

The notes just described may be studied in tablature.

Ex.15   Or

B *fa*, B *mi* remains to be harmonized.

Ex.16

It is set apart because one must note that B *mi* does not have a perfect fifth in the natural keys; its fifth is F *fa ut,* and this fifth, which is called a false fifth, is a dissonance. Therefore, for now, learn to harmonize B *mi* with a sixth, playing an octave in the left hand without touching any key in between. The right hand may place its index finger on D, which will be a third; its fourth finger on G, which will be a sixth; and its little finger on B, which will be another octave; or may move higher, playing (with the same fingers) G,B,D, which will be the sixth, the octave, and the third.

Ex.17   Or   Fuller
                                                    With the sixth in the middle

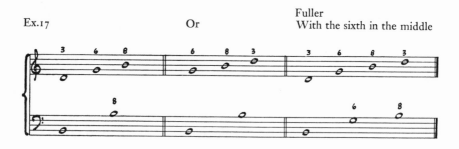

In this manner one goes about acquiring knowledge and skill with the consonances, taking care to play the notes on the proper key and string, as they are written and not at the octave above or below, but every one in its proper register. For example, when the notes are found in the acute octave, as in the following,

Ex.18

they are to be played with the consonances in close position, it being sufficient if the left hand forms only a third, or sometimes just the note itself, but with all the necessary consonances in the right hand—that is, the third, the fifth, and the octave, or in the case of B *mi* the sixth. When the student is proficient one does not mind if he sometimes doubles the notes at the octave—this on the authority of the experts.

The teacher will not fail to find a way of showing the beginning student how best to assure keeping time when playing certain notes of longer duration, for example of a measure or half-measure in length.[4] One can repeat the note every quarter, or fill out the measure by playing an octave in the left hand, or some other note in between, such as the third, fifth, or sixth.

Ex.19 (a)

(b)

____

[4] The original reads "una, o mezza battuta." See the Foreword.

In triple time the same is done with notes that last a whole measure, or for two counts, or are syncopated.[5]

Ex.20   (a)

(b)

In any case, the student must properly understand the beat.

CHAPTER III

Musical Accidentals

I HAVE USED LEAPS IN THE PRECEDING EXAMPLES BECAUSE in that way they work well with simple consonances, are not subject so easily to the errors of two fifths and two octaves, and do not require different kinds of accompaniment nor any accidentals. It is now necessary to know about the musical accidentals, or accidental signs, and their uses. These are the semitones, which are of three sorts, namely flat, natural, and sharp.[6] These serve, for our purposes, for passing from a white key to a black one, either ascending or descending. The effect of the flat is to lower the note a semitone (or half tone), of the sharp to raise it, and of the natural to return it to its natural place after having been altered by a flat. The latter applies to the three notes B *mi*, E *la mi*, and A *la mi re*. Note that B *fa*, B *mi* with the flat is called B *fa*, and without it B *mi*.

Notice that between all the notes, that is, from one to the next, or from one key to another, there is normally the interval of a whole tone, except that from *mi* to *fa*, that is from E to F and from B to C, there is only a half tone. The three notes indicated by the clefs, F,C, and G, normally have a major third above them that is subject to being made minor with the accidental flat. The other four notes, A,B,D, and E, normally

---

[6] Gasparini has "cioè b.molle ♭, b.quadro ♮, e [diesis] ♯"; here the term "diesis" is omitted. See the Foreword.

have a minor third above them that is subject to being made major with the accidental sharp. A,B, and E have a minor sixth, and C,D,F, and G have a major sixth, subject to the same modifications by these same accidentals.

The sharp placed next to a note raises it a half tone, which means that instead of the white key, one plays the black key next above in order to ascend. The flat has the opposite effect, and the natural returns the note to its natural place.

Ex.21   *Effect of the sharp*

Effect of the flat and natural

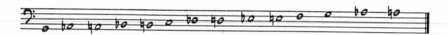

Another example, descending with flat and sharp

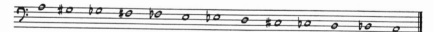

Notice that the flat serves also to cancel the sharp of a note previously altered by it; in this case the flat does not lower the note, but returns it to its natural place.

When the sharp is found placed above or below the note, it indicates a major third; the flat, a minor third. Likewise, placed next to a number these accidentals have the same effect on that consonance (perfect or imperfect) or dissonance, as the case may be.

Ex.22

When these accidentals are found at the beginning of the staff next to the clef, the pitches on which they are located, whether used as fundamental notes or as accompaniments, are altered accordingly, becoming black keys.

Ex.23

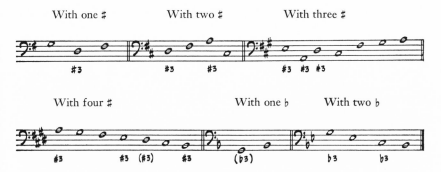

From this it is clear that any note marked with an accidental sign at the clef must be played with that accidental.

CHAPTER IV

Remarks on Ascending Motion, First by Step [And Later by Leap]

WHEN NOTES ASCEND BY STEP, SEEING THAT TWO PERFECT consonances of the same kind are prohibited in parallel motion, one can play a sixth after each fifth, thus avoiding the progression of two fifths.

Ex.24

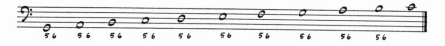

When a note ascends a semitone, either natural or accidental (as in the following from E to F, from B to C, from F-sharp to G, from A to B-flat, and in similar instances) the first note takes a minor sixth.

Ex.25

Or one may play the sixth followed by a diminished fifth, and sometimes the two together.

Ex.26

When a note that ascends a semitone has either a natural or accidental major third above it, then do not play a sixth with it (unless either indicated, or found in the upper, written part); the following note usually calls for a natural major sixth.

Ex.27

And when the composition calls for a sixth, either directly or through resolution, together with the said major third, then the following note may have a fifth, and sometimes the fifth followed by a sixth.

Ex.28 [7]

With the direct sixth   With the sixth as a resolution

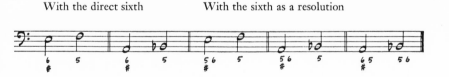

In these stepwise progressions it is very easy to fall into the error of two fifths or two octaves. To avoid them, make use of contrary motion as much as possible, particularly when the outermost finger of the right hand (that is to say, the highest key) forms either a fifth or an octave with the bass. One cannot go wrong using a tenth in the highest part, or a sixth when necessary.

[7] We have exchanged the last two instances of Ex.28; later editions, e.g. the fifth, change 65 to the easier reading 56.

In accompanying quarter-notes, or eighth-notes, one is certain to meet with much difficulty, particularly when moving by step. Without a great deal of practice and knowledge of counterpoint I judge it difficult, though not impossible, not to err in the consonances or create bad intervallic relations. It is true, however, that many (in accordance with contrapuntal practice) give it as a rule that one should treat one note as essential and the next as unessential,[8] that is to say, accompany one note with the appropriate consonances and pass over the next, playing only the bass. This would be worthwhile to observe on the organ; but because it seems to produce a dry, sparse effect on the harpsichord, it is better to accompany each note with its own appropriate harmony, which will be easy with the help of the remarks given here for the purpose.

Now if the composition begins with three quarter-notes ascending stepwise, or two quarter-notes followed by notes of other values, the first will be harmonized according to the rule of the simple consonances, the second with a major sixth, and the third with a natural sixth.

Ex.29

If after the three quarter-notes the same notes are repeated one step higher, the note that was given a major sixth the first time is given a minor sixth the second. Study this example carefully.

Ex.30 [9]

[8] Gasparini wrote "una buona e una cattiva."

[9] In the last measure of Ex.30, the first edition places the sharp over the last note.

If four quarter-notes ascend by step in common time,[10] one can accompany the first fully, and as for the others it is highly effective to hold the note that forms an octave with the first note, giving them all the third or tenth. But where there is an initial rest they are all to be harmonized fully, with a natural sixth for the two in the middle.

Ex.31

With a quarter-rest before

Where there are five notes ascending by step, one can play them like the four notes above, or in the way shown in the following example.

Ex.32

How to gain assurance in the correct way of accompanying the notes named above, and any stepwise progression, will emerge from remarks to be made in Chapter VIII.

Eighth-notes can be considered like quarter-notes, except that in some faster tempos it is permissible to accompany them alternately, considering one essential and the next unessential, both ascending and descending. This is easier for the beginner, while the expert will use his judgment and discretion in the matter of tempos and progressions.

[10] Gasparini wrote "in tempo perfetto, o binario." See the Foreword, and translator's note at Ex.62 further on.

Note that when either the downbeat or the upbeat of a measure begins with an eighth-rest, the three eighth-notes of that half measure must be accompanied, because one cannot treat the eighth-note that begins each fourth of the measure as unessential.

Ex.33

With an eighth-rest before

The same procedure is used if in place of the eighth-rest there is another note that does not move by step.

Ex.34

In proportional measures, such as triple, sextuple, sesquialtera, etc., one can pass over the middle note of the three in each measure, making sure to accompany properly the one that is on the downbeat.

Ex.35

In rapid tempos it is also possible to accompany the first and pass over the other two.

Sixteenth-notes are passed over four at a time when they occur step-wise, whether ascending or descending, and one may also pass over some leaps of a third. It is sufficient to accompany, or harmonize fully, the first sixteenth-note of every quarter of the measure.

Ex.36

When there are various leaps of a fourth, fifth, sixth, or octave, they are to be accompanied two at a time, that is to say, one is accompanied and the next not.

Ex.37

When there is a sixteenth-rest, it is effective for the right hand to play the consonances of the first note of that beat while the left hand rests.

Ex.38

Ascending by Leaps of a Third

A sixth is ordinarily added to the note that follows a leap of a third, whether the third is major or minor.

Ex.39

Major third   Minor third

If the preceding note must carry a sixth, the following calls for a fifth.

Ex.40

Major third   Minor third

Whenever one finds a sharp before the second note of this leap, it receives a sixth, and the preceding note a major third.

Ex.41

When after this leap, either major or minor, there follows a leap of a fifth down or of a fourth up, which is called the cadential leap, then one gives to the first note its natural sixth, and to the second a major third.

Ex.42

And when after the leap of a third there follow two or more leaps of a fourth up or a fifth down, then all are accompanied by the simple consonances without any accidentals. But for this it would be better to proceed to the study of leaps of a fourth and a fifth.

Ascending by Leaps of a Fourth

The rule generally given for the leap of a fourth up is that, like the leap of a fifth down, it calls for a major third. But I note that it may be dangerous to adopt this rule unconditionally, because this leap is found in many situations that require a minor third. It will therefore be made clear later on, where I illustrate the way of modulating from key to key, how to use a major third only where it is required. For now, study the following example.

Ex.43

Here one sees ascending leaps of a fourth that never call for a major third except where it comes naturally, and where a cadence is formed by the leap of a fifth down. In fact, it must be observed that when finding many of these leaps together one must never use the major third except where it falls naturally, and then for the final leap forming the cadence. If all except the first, which begins the series of leaps, and the last, which terminates them, have the seventh added, it will be very effective. Make sure that every seventh is tied over from the preceding chord, noting that the third of one becomes the seventh of the next.

Ex.44

Do not use a fifth with the note that follows the leap of a diminished, or false, fifth, because it produces a bad relation. The third and seventh are sufficient.

Ex.45

This observation will be better understood from some examples in Chapter VII.

The leap of a fifth up will be studied for now only in long note values, that is, values of a measure or half measure. After playing the third and fifth, resolve to a fourth and major sixth. Do the same when descending a fourth.

Ex.46

This rule is very useful for certain plagal cadences used in church music.

The note that ordinarily follows this leap in certain compositions of a quicker tempo calls for a major third.

Ex.47

It is necessary to observe that relationships sometimes do not permit a major third with the leap just mentioned. One can tell from the corresponding natural notes, as here.

Ex.48

The ascending leap of a sixth may be considered as a descending leap of a third, and will be treated in the next chapter.

CHAPTER V

Remarks on Descending by Step and by Leap

WHEN DESCENDING STEPWISE IN LONG NOTES, GIVE THE first note a fifth and then a sixth. To all the others give a seventh resolved with the natural sixth, except the last which must always have a major sixth.

Ex.49

A single note descending stepwise receives a fifth followed by a major sixth, or a seventh followed by a sixth, or sometimes the major sixth only.

Ex.50

For the most part, where there are many notes descending stepwise, the last note receives a major sixth, being a kind of cadence; for in a certain sense that note is interpreted as bringing about a modulation to the note following—provided the bass then moves in some other manner, either ascending stepwise or leaping in various ways. It is necessary to give no little thought to this example.

Ex.51

When descending stepwise in half-notes and quarter-notes, notice that when one note has the simple consonances, the next calls for a sixth. Following is an example of two notes that descend stepwise.

Ex.52

An example of three quarter-notes, or three notes of different values, moving stepwise:

Ex.53

When the first of the three takes a major third, and the second descends a whole tone, pass over it completely. It is very effective to play along with it the same keys as for the first note, resulting in a second, an augmented fourth, and a sixth. The following note gets a natural sixth.

Ex.54

If the middle note descends a semitone it takes a third and a sixth, most often a minor or natural sixth. However, one can tell from the composition, or from the progressions noted in the examples above, when it must be major.

Examples of four quarter-notes, or four notes of different values, moving stepwise:

Ex.55

In this one may observe the same rules as above: *mi* before or after *fa* takes a sixth, and every cadence that descends stepwise a major sixth. Sometimes one proceeds with sixths alone, but this, for the most part, will be indicated in the composition itself, either by the figures or by the upper part.

With eighth-notes one observes the rule given above of one note essential and the next unessential, making frequent use of tenths, and playing the fourth eighth-note with a major sixth on either upbeat or downbeat.

Ex.56

When descending a leap of a third, if the first note is harmonized with the simple consonances and if after the leap the motion is stepwise, then the second note takes a sixth. If the continuation is by leap, use the simple consonances.

Ex.57

If the first note takes a major third, the next takes a sixth, regardless of any leap that may follow. However, this rule applies without exception only when the leap is a major third, that is, two whole tones; for when the leap is a minor third, that is, a whole tone and a semitone, then the second note sometimes calls for a fifth—but, subject to the progression, one observes the rules indicated above.

Ex.58

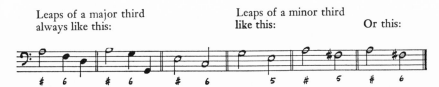

Sometimes the composition forms a kind of cadence, coming to rest on a note with its major third, and then makes a new start, moving to the third below. In such cases, that note calls not for a sixth, but a fifth.

Ex.59

This is found in sacred as well as secular vocal compositions, both for the chamber and for the theater, in which it is used to end an interrogative or exclamatory phrase and then to begin the next; it is usually found in the serious style, or in recitative.

If the note that leaps a third, either major or minor, takes a sixth, the next is given the simple consonances, without moving the right hand.

Ex.60

A descending leap of a fourth is treated like an ascending leap of a fifth. Likewise, a descending leap of a fifth is treated like an ascending leap of a fourth, since they are complementary, in that they move to notes that have the same sound, that is, the octave. For the same reason the descending leap of a sixth is considered as an ascending leap of a third, and vice versa.

But let us not pass over the leap of a descending fifth without discussing the cadences, since most cadences are formed with this leap.

CHAPTER VI

How to Make Cadences
of All Kinds

CADENCES ARE PRINCIPALLY OF TWO KINDS, SIMPLE AND compound. Simple cadences are formed in two ways, one with a major third descending a leap of a fifth or ascending a leap of a fourth, the other with a major sixth descending stepwise.

Ex.61 *Simple cadences*

By leap   By step

There are four kinds of compound cadences: greater, lesser, diminished, and deceptive.

The greater cadence is formed in common time,[11] using four counts, in the following way. On the first count give the note the simple consonances with the major third. On the second count play the fourth and

---

[11] Gasparini has "in tempo perfetto." See the Foreword, and translator's note at Ex.31 above.

sixth. On the third count play the fifth together with the fourth. On the fourth and last count, resolve the fourth to a major third, and on the same count (the last eighth of the measure) add the seventh, which then descends one step to the third or tenth above the next bass note, ending the cadence.

Ex.62   *Greater compound cadences*

Often these cadences are anticipated with a tied seventh in the following way.

Ex.63

Notice that in these greater cadences the accompaniments indicated here are always required, even though for the most part one finds no figures with the note except for 3,4,3 or 7,6,5, and sometimes nothing at all.

In triple time, two measures are needed to form the cadence.

Ex.64

By lesser cadence is meant shorter in time. This cadence is formed with the fourth resolved by the major third; the fifth is played together with the fourth. But for the most part—particularly in chamber works for solo voice—the fourth goes well with the sixth, which is resolved to a fifth when the fourth resolves to a third. Playing the seventh at the same time creates an excellent effect.

Ex.65 [12] *Lesser cadences*

The diminished cadences are several. They derive from the greater and lesser cadences, since the note forming the cadence is divided into two, four, or more notes. Several examples are shown here.

Ex.66 [13]

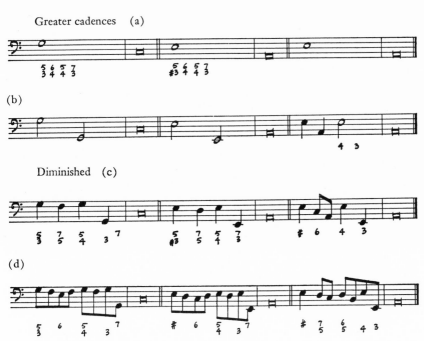

Greater cadences   (a)

(b)

Diminished   (c)

(d)

[12] In Ex.65, the cadence on C reads (in the first edition): barline, C-half, G-half, C-quarter, G-quarter, barline. In the sixth edition the second C is made a whole-note, the second G omitted. We have made a more elaborate emendation.

[13] In Ex.66c, the first edition gives the figures $\frac{6}{5}$ for the first note.

Most of the diminished lesser cadences are similar to the greater cadences, with the single difference that they last only a half measure. They are formed in many ways, as the following examples show.

Ex.67   *Lesser cadences with fourth and fifth resolved to a third*

Other cadences with fourth and sixth resolved to third and fifth

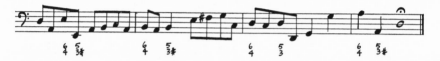

The method of resolving these cadences of the fourth and sixth is very easy, because when the right hand is properly placed, playing the fourth, sixth, and octave, it is not necessary to do anything but descend one step with each finger. In this way the fourth descends to a major third, the sixth to a fifth, and the octave to a seventh.

Sometimes doubling the fourth and sixth in the left hand produces a very good effect, but in the resolution one must not allow the major third to be heard. On the harpsichord, leaving the fourth to sound together with the fifth while resolving to the major third in the right hand produces a most pleasing harmony; it is a kind of *acciaccatura*, as many performers call it, an effect that will be discussed separately later on. This, however, does not work well on the organ, except in full, thick texture.

When the cadence is to fall on some middle note, such as C *sol fa ut*, D *la sol re*, or E *la mi* (so called because in the customary clef of F *fa ut* these notes occupy the middle of the staff,

Ex.68   Ex.69

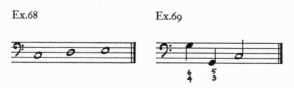

and also because of their position in the middle of the keyboard on the harpsichord) it is both easy and effective to play as follows. If G *sol re ut* is to resolve to C *sol fa ut* (Ex.69), then place the index finger on E-acute, which makes a sixth, the middle finger on the G above, which makes an octave, and the little finger on the following C, which makes a fourth. Then resolve by moving each finger down one step, so that the cadence may be, as said above, well prepared and resolved; to end on C *sol fa ut*, move the hand back up stepwise to the same keys as before. Along with the seventh one may add an octave with the ring finger, so that the harmony may be fuller and more sonorous. The other two cadences on D *la sol re* and E *la mi* are formed in the same manner. Satisfy yourself at the instrument how easy this is; here are the three cadences.

Ex.70

Note that the resolved third of the cadence is always major, and that the fifth of B *mi* is raised a semitone to become the sharp of F *fa ut*.

Using the same hand-position, the same cadence is sometimes formed with a fifth instead of the sixth, playing this fifth with the thumb of the left hand, as is more convenient. Also with this same hand-position, one can successfully play the greater cadences in the middle positions described above. See them in tablature.

Ex.71

Greater cadence Lesser cadence

In the compound cadence formed by descending stepwise there is no distinction between greater or lesser forms, because, whether the note that prepares it is of larger or smaller value, nothing more is required than the seventh resolved to the major sixth, as shown below.

Ex.72 *Simple stepwise cadences*

Diminished cadences are formed in this manner:

Ex.73

Deceptive cadences are formed in different ways. They are called deceptive when the composition containing the cadence does not terminate on the usual notes, but moves in an unexpected way to another unanticipated chord or note. A cadence is also called deceptive when the resolution is minor instead of major; this, however, would be indicated in the figures or in the upper composed part.

Ex.74 *Deceptive cadences*

At this point it seems to me that I have said enough about cadences.

The teacher must now show the student, little by little, the accidentals for all the keys that have sharps or flats in the scale; then the industrious student will be able to occupy himself in seeking out and practicing these cadences over the whole keyboard, being guided by the standard forms given in the examples above.

CHAPTER VII

Dissonances, Ties, Syncopations, and How to Resolve Them

Among the musical intervals, as mentioned in Chapter I, there are the dissonances. Just as these are often used in harmonic composition for the sake of their great beauty and charm, and for the unusual pleasure they bring to the listener when they are properly prepared and resolved, so, too, it is necessary to make use of them in accompanying, knowing how to prepare, tie, and resolve them in accord with the composed parts.

They are called dissonances because they produce discordant sounds, described as such by the ancients, who not only found them false, harsh, and displeasing to the ear, but judged them so also by well-founded reasons of nature; we will not seek explanations other than those which the curious reader may find in Boethius, or in many other well-known writers on this subject. It will suffice for our purpose to know that the dissonances are the second, the fourth, the diminished or false fifth, the seventh, and the ninth. These are considered the same in their doublings at the acute or at the superacute octave, being compound or doubly compound like the consonances.

The ancients placed the fourth among the perfect consonances: one reads in very many authors that the first intervals to be used were the *diatessaron, diapente,* and *diapason,* that is, the fourth, fifth, and octave. And in fact the fourth, placed among the consonances, is considered by both the ancients and the moderns as a perfect consonance, but was not approved for use as a foundation. So, for this reason and for our purposes, we shall call it a dissonance; it must be used with its tie and resolution like the other dissonances.

Above those notes where one finds written the figures mentioned earlier (2, 4, ♭5, 7, 9), one must notice that the added part is tied over from the preceding note; hence the note preceding the one that has the sign of the dissonance has above it the very note that is to serve as a dissonance for the next note. One must see to it, therefore, that the hand does not leave or depart from that position, and specifically that the finger, remaining on that same key found over the said preceding note, must then resolve to the nearest consonance, descending stepwise. Usually the fourth resolves to a third, the seventh to a sixth, and the ninth to an octave; but I shall illustrate everything more precisely.

The second may be considered the same as the ninth, since the ninth is the compound of the second, and because ordinarily one indicates a second and the interval will be a ninth. There is, however, a notable difference between the two, since the second does not derive from, but proceeds to a tie, that is to say, when the bass is tied or syncopated. In this case the second does not resolve, as do the other dissonances, but instead the bass itself resolves stepwise downward.

Ex.75

The second, then, must be played on the second count of the tied or syncopated note, and when the preceding note, to which it is tied, is of

longer value, notice that the second is played on either half of the measure. Notice, too, that a fourth is required along with the second, either
augmented or perfect as it falls naturally, or as the composition indicates
through the use of accidentals.

Ex.76

Sometimes one finds repeated notes, in which case one should play the
second and fourth with those that come at the beginning of every half
measure, whether downbeat or upbeat, exactly as in the case of tied values.

Ex.77

These are treated as if they were tied in the following way.

Ex.78

After these and similar ties the note that descends stepwise usually
calls for a sixth, particularly when the fourth is augmented. Furthermore, the sixth is always desirable along with the second and the fourth
as well. All of this applies even if the tied or syncopated note has no sign,
or has only one, either the second, fourth, or sixth, because on such occasions one does not play one without the other. An exception occurs when
a syncopated note in the bass does not have a descending resolution but is

followed by some other note, ascending either stepwise or by leap, as will be seen in the example below. In such cases one plays either a sixth or the simple consonances with the syncopated note.

Ex.79

If a second is found tied like a ninth, which resolves to the octave, the second should be resolved to a unison. But since the keyboard is not adapted to it, such a resolution would not be heard. For this reason, when such ties are needed (which is rare in harmonic composition) one can use a ninth instead, which is more distinctly resolved to an octave—as will be seen in the proper place.

In *cantilene* one finds—though rarely—a certain passage using the augmented fourth and a sixth. See the following example of it, giving the upper part.

Ex.80

This sort of augmented second is usual in certain preparations for cadences, and for expressing melancholy words, etc. So much for the practice and study of the second.

The fourth is, as mentioned, a consonance when it occurs among the upper parts, but placed next to the bass it is considered a dissonance. For this reason it, too, must be tied over, or be played together with a second above a tied-over bass, as already shown. The fourth serves for cadences and is resolved to a third; it calls for a fifth added above it, and often a sixth, as demonstrated in the cadences of Chapter V.

The augmented fourth, otherwise called the tritone, is always a dissonance. It was not used by the ancient musicians, being considered harsh and intolerable. But it is much used by modern composers, for when treated properly and with good taste it becomes very sweet and harmonious, provided it is resolved correctly. The augmented fourth is always placed together with the second and the major sixth, as mentioned before.

The diminished, or false, fifth is a dissonance. It is similar to the tritone with the difference that the tritone consists of three tones, the diminished fifth of two tones and two semitones. There is also this difference, that the tritone, or augmented fourth, comprises four steps, the diminished fifth five.

Ex.81

(a)   Tritones

(b)   Diminished fifths

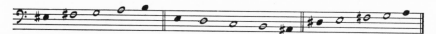

This diminished fifth as used in the accompaniment may occur either tied or untied. It may not be resolved in the manner of the other dissonances, since it would resolve to a fourth. Instead, when the bass moves, the note above must descend to form a third, that is, the note that has over it this false fifth ascends stepwise a semitone, and when the false fifth descends stepwise, the result is a third, either major or minor according to the composition.

Ex.82

To the diminished fifth must always be joined a third, and often a sixth—

especially when using long note-values, in which case the sixth is required—provided there is no seventh tied over.

Ordinarily when the bass forms a false fifth it will ascend stepwise. But sometimes the bass note proceeds to a diminution two, three, four, or more notes in length, throughout which it is necessary to hold the key that was the diminished fifth at the beginning until the arrival of the note that forms the third for the resolution of the diminished fifth. Study the example carefully.

Ex.83 [14]

It is excellent practice to derive another dissonance from the false fifth. Take care in such cases to hold the tied note until the resolution of the new dissonance. See the example with the composed part.

Ex.84

It is customary in compositions for several voices to use a few ties in the upper parts where they are linked with one another by dissonances of a second or seventh. In relation to one another they resolve regularly, but are always consonant with the bass. They occur when the fifth and sixth are indicated together, as $\frac{5}{6}$ or $\frac{6}{5}$. The third is always necessary; its

[14] For the third note of the third measure of Ex.83, the first edition gives A, which, however, is not out of the question; in the same measure (and the next) the tie in the first edition includes only the last three notes before the bar.

resolution depends on that of the fifth, which, in descending one key, will resolve (for the most part) to a third. At the same time the bass ascends stepwise or by leap, according to its movements, as the example demonstrates.

Ex.85

Of all the dissonances, the seventh is the most frequent since it has three forms, all used in composition. In order to distinguish them we shall call the first the major seventh, the second the minor seventh, and the third the diminished or imperfect seventh. In speaking of the seventh, however, we do not refer to it as major or minor unless accidentals make it necessary to do so. It will ordinarily be referred to as a seventh, understanding thereby the natural seventh. The first, the major seventh, is composed of five whole tones and a semitone; more simply, it is the one that lacks only a semitone of being an octave.

Ex.86

Natural major sevenths

Major sevenths
using accidentals

But we call major only those sevenths formed with sharps. Notes with flats also have the major seventh, but here they are called natural sevenths.

Ex.87

Natural major sevenths using a flat

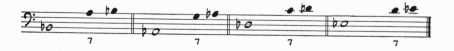

The second seventh, which we shall call minor, is the one composed of four tones and two semitones, and lacks a whole tone of being an octave.

Ex.88

Natural minor sevenths

Minor sevenths using accidentals

The third seventh, which is called imperfect, has the same interval as the major sixth, and is composed of three tones and three semitones. It lacks a tone and a half of being an octave. But for the sake of clarity it will always be called the minor seventh.

Ex.89

All three are called sevenths because they are made up of seven steps.

Ex.90

| Major seventh | Minor seventh | Imperfect seventh |

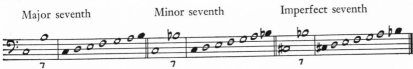

The major and minor sevenths will be so called on the basis of their use of accidentals; but when they are natural it will not be necessary in our usage to give them any special name.

Generally the seventh must never be without a third. It may also have the fifth, but one must distinguish clearly where and when, as we shall show by examples. To begin with, the seventh is tied in the upper part to a preceding note, and it must resolve to the major sixth—as ordinarily happens in the stepwise cadence. But when there are several successive notes occurring stepwise that call for a seventh and a sixth, only the final one is resolved with the raised sixth.

Ex.91

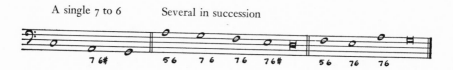

When descending stepwise in longer note-values (a half-note or longer) one can add a fifth along with the seventh, but the fifth must be released immediately with the resolution to the sixth; in its place one can double the third or sixth, as best suits the hand. First, however, I would advise the student to master this tied seventh without the fifth, since it is not always necessary. It must also be pointed out that some fifths stand in a bad relationship with the bass note, particularly in the case of B *mi* and those notes with a sharp, and are therefore to be avoided.

Ex.92

And although in some cadential leaps, namely those of a fifth down or a fourth up, it is necessary to join the fifth to the seventh, nevertheless in those cases where it does not occur properly and naturally, or correctly prepared by the accidentals, it must be avoided.

Ex.93

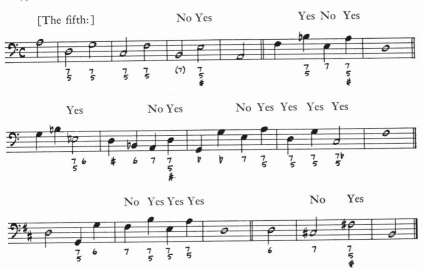

Study these common progressions that require a seventh even when it is not indicated, considering carefully where to omit the fifth.

Ex.94

The fifth:

The diligent student can continue in this fashion, studying each key and genus, and observing carefully that if the first note (of the example) has a minor third, then the note with a seventh does not take a fifth, but does if the first note has a major third. Similarly, as a general rule, a fifth is used with the seventh each time it occurs with a major third, especially over the note that leads into a cadence.

In some bass progressions the seventh may resolve to a third or fifth—with the condition that, in order to be correct, the resolution must descend stepwise from the seventh, falling on the next adjacent key.

Ex.95

There are some cadences, much in use, that are preceded by two leaps, one descending a third, the other ascending a fourth. The first note takes a fifth and sixth, and the second note a seventh. If the first note has a major third, the other, which has the seventh, may take a fifth; otherwise it may not, for the reasons mentioned above.

Ex.96

The fifth:

The seventh often serves for a particular anticipation of the cadence. When there is a note a tone or semitone below the one leading to the cadence, and when this note has a seventh, either tied over or direct, then it always receives a fifth. Even if it is altered by a sharp and the fifth is false, still this fifth is desirable and, indeed, very effective.

Ex.97

In this anticipation of the cadence with the tied seventh, even when the seventh resolves to a sixth, the fifth must remain along with the sixth.

Ex.98

These examples, if well practiced, will prove very useful.

The imperfect seventh, which we shall always call "minor," is much used by modern composers, but particularly for two sorts of very delightful and expressive passages, especially in recitatives. I shall demonstrate this clearly with examples. Now the two ways in which this "minor" seventh is used are these: in the first the bass ascends a semitone; in the second it descends a semitone. In the first, this seventh calls for a third along with it, which will be naturally minor, and a diminished fifth. The bass then leads into the note a step above, which is harmonized by the simple consonances.

Ex.99

The fuller one can make these chords, the more harmony they will produce. Be sure, however, to double all the notes, which is easy if one plays all the notes in the left hand, that is, the principal note, the third, fifth, and seventh, and then doubles them in the same way in the right hand an octave higher.

This seventh may be found either tied or direct. When it is tied, it generally resolves above the same bass note to a sixth, retaining the diminished fifth and the third, as shown in the last example but one (Ex.98); see also the following example.

Ex.100

The second passage where one meets this "minor" seventh is simply the tied seventh resolved to a sixth over a bass descending by semitones.

Ex.101

Here the seventh should not have the fifth but always the third

The ninth, although of two kinds, one a whole tone and the other a semitone above the octave, is not called major or minor, because the composition inevitably shows which it is by the appropriate accidentals. For clarity, however, the first ninth may be called just and the other minor because, while they both require a third or tenth, the just ninth requires a fifth, but the minor ninth does not. This is because—as must be pointed out—the fifth forms a false relationship with the note that is the ninth, a semitone above the octave, and so must be avoided. In its place the minor sixth may be used, although it is not absolutely necessary.

Even though the ninth is the equivalent of the second, being a compound second, still it is treated differently. It is never used without a tie: in contrast to the second, which occurs over a tie in the lower part (the bass), the ninth itself is tied in the upper part in order to be resolved to the octave.

Ex.102

Just ninths

If the ninth is minor, the fifth is not used, except that when ascending stepwise for several notes the fifth and sixth may be used, or sometimes only the sixth; or the sixth may enter with the octave resolution of the ninth.

Ex.103

Ninths: Minor   Just   Minor

Two tied notes are sometimes found together, as for example the ninth and the seventh. In such cases each requires its proper resolution, and the chord always has a third or tenth.

Ex.104

The ninth may also be used tied over along with the fourth. Here the fifth is used, and not the third, because the third occurs as the resolution of the fourth.

Ex.105

In diminutions of the bass the ninth may be resolved by any other consonance, that is to say by the third, fifth, or sixth, provided that the resolution correctly descends to the key next below, like the resolution of the seventh when the bass moves to a note other than the usual one.

This practice, followed by the better modern composers, is found particularly in the extremely delightful *Sinfonie* of Arcangelo Corelli, supreme virtuoso of the violin, true Orpheus of our time, who moves and shifts his basses with so much artfulness, care, and grace, using these ties and dissonances, so well controlled and resolved, and so well interwoven with a variety of themes, that one may well say he has rediscovered the perfection of ravishing harmony. And I could go on—except that it would divert us from our purpose, and I would, I fear, be regarded as of small wit, going out of my way to speak of one so well known by reputation and by his own magnificent accomplishments. But whoever undertakes to practice using the basses of his compositions will derive great benefit thereby, and will attain the highest skill in every style of accompaniment.

Study the following examples; with tied-over notes of this kind endeavor to make the resolutions carefully and judiciously, keeping the right hand in close position and moving it for the most part in a descending direction. This will be easier to do if the first ties are played by the uppermost finger, which is to say, in the highest part.

Ex.106

Be sure to treat the second eighth-note of every four as unessential even though it may be approached by a leap, applying the rules given above in Chapter IV concerning the accompaniment of stepwise quarter- and eighth-notes. Here is another example of double ties above diminutions of the bass:

Ex.107

Another progression, in which the ninth is resolved to a third:

Ex.108

It will help to remember that, with dissonances of any sort, the same finger that plays the suspension, namely the finger that strikes the note creating the dissonance, also plays its resolution. Try always to use the right hand in forming the ties, and in joining them to the consonances already discussed.

CHAPTER VIII

Remarks on How Best to Master Accompaniment in Every Key: How to Modulate Well, Anticipate, and Pass Properly from One Key to Another

THE FIRST THING ONE MUST DETERMINE ABOUT ANY COM-
position to be accompanied is the mode [15] in which it is written, or at least
(without entering into the difficulties of the modes, that is, of the first,
second, third, etc.) to know precisely on which note the piece is composed. Because of the variety of melodic figures, the bass does not always
begin with the proper fundamental note on which the composition is
formed and on which it must end. This is particularly true in the basses

[15] The original has "Tono." See the Foreword.

of arias for either one or two voices. If the bass begins with a thematic figure, one may often have doubts about the proper accompaniments— unless it begins with precisely the note on which it ends. But even without extensive knowledge and experience, one can tell this immediately by looking at the first cadence, or, to be absolutely sure, at the last. For instance, a motif may begin with the upper fifth, as in the following example.

Ex.109

This is called beginning with the upper fifth because the first note is A *la mi re* and the cadence ends on D *la sol re*.

From the rules already given one could tell immediately what accompaniments these notes require. While A, leaping down a fifth, requires the major third, D, as the first half of the second count of the measure, naturally has the simple consonances. E, being reached by step, is passed over as unessential. F will take its sixth, according to the rule for ascending stepwise and because of its relationship to D. G will take a fifth and a sixth. A will again take a major third because of its relationship to the first A—and similarly the other notes that follow will conform to the rules already given. But since it is very difficult to retain so many things in the memory, I will proceed to illustrate a number of points for facilitating their mastery; but particular attention is here required.

It would seem that I ought here to describe the characteristics and the number of the modes and their formation. But this is a subject requiring a lengthy treatise, better adapted to the needs of a student of counterpoint; moreover it has been sufficiently treated by numerous well-known authors, among whose works the student will find what he needs. In order not to dwell too long on what is not essential for us, and in order not to inflict on the mind a double burden, I have hit upon a device that will permit my ingenious player to understand without too much confusion what is involved in the treatment of each key [16] with its proper accompaniments. It suffices to state that any composition whatsoever is formed either with the major third or with the minor. This becomes immediately evident in reading the notes. In the case of a major third, starting from precisely that note on which the composition is built, read: *ut, re, mi;* in the case of a minor third: *re, mi, fa.* I leave out consideration of the third and fourth modes, which must be read: *mi, fa, sol,* since this is not applied rigorously by present-day composers with its original structure, but with transpositions that would make explanations necessary. I shall revert to common, accepted practice in order not to deviate from our subject. Study, then, examples of every key, beginning with those with the major third.

Ex.110 [17]

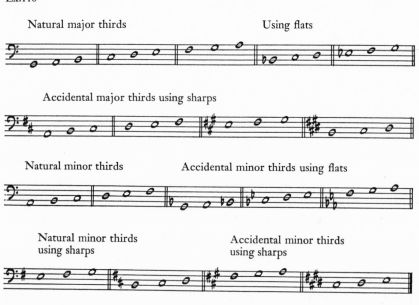

Notice in all these cases that—either naturally, or by the use of accidentals—one may read *do, re, mi* for the major and *re, mi, fa* for the minor,

---

[16] The original has "Tono." See the Foreword.

[17] The first title of Ex.110 reads "Terze minori naturali" in the first edition.

since the flat changes the note, giving it the nature of *fa*, and the sharp, on the other hand, changes it by giving it the nature of *mi*.

In the rules for ascending stepwise already given in Chapter IV one may discover how to provide correct accompaniments. But in changing and varying the keys and in modulating abruptly, one needs further instructions, which I shall explain little by little with examples.

Having recognized at the outset the principal note of the key in which the composition is written—G *sol re ut* for example—notice the major accidental employed at its cadences, a major third above D *la sol re* and a major sixth above A *la mi re*. This will be the black key above F, which is the semitone next below G. Therefore in every accompaniment in which F may enter one must always play it with the sharp, avoiding the natural, except when the latter is explicitly written in the bass. For the bass, that is, the foundation and basis of the harmony, is to be considered as the master, while the accompaniments (the consonances) are as servants subject to it. And so, as stated before, give the major sixth to the note next above the fundamental prime of the key. Here another observation is necessary—an easy one. When moving from the raised semitone never descend, but always ascend. For example, imagine that the composition is in the key of A *la mi re*. The sharp called for by its cadences will be G-sharp, so that G-natural is to be avoided in the accompaniments. Thus the major sixth, G-sharp, that one gives to the first note ascending stepwise from A (which will be B) can then only ascend a semitone, to A.

The other observation concerns the notes that customarily form the cadence in a key. There are principally two: one is its (the key's) neighbor a whole tone above, the other the fifth above or the fourth below. For example, in relation to A the first will be B, the second E. The B requires a major sixth, the E always a major third—unless the bass invalidates this rule by passing into other keys through the formation of other cadences, or unless there are other indications in the composed part, or (as in the following example) in the figures or accidentals.

Ex.112

Here the key has been changed from A *la mi re* to G *sol re ut*. This is shown by the sixth indicated for the last B, preparing the cadence of D descending to G. When the G-sharp returns it will be a sign that the key has returned to A.

Ex.113

From this it is understood that every key has its required accidental, which is the major third of the chord preceding the cadence, and this same sharp is sufficient to identify the key. Thus if one sees E with a major third, one recognizes immediately that the key is A. Remove that accidental sharp and it is a sign that the key is changed. There is another observation to be made about intervals within keys: if the key is one with a minor third, that is, with *re, mi, fa*, the note a fourth above the key also requires a minor third. At that point there occurs the same pattern, *re, mi, fa*. This can be seen in the following example.

Ex.114

Therefore, when that note (a fourth above) is reached, whether by step or by leap, it will always call for a minor third.

Ex.115 [18]   (a)

(b)

From this, then, we can be sure which consonances the notes require, even when the bass begins its figure on a note other than the principal note of the key. After careful study of the first example in this chapter, one can figure out similar solutions for the other keys, applying the same accidentals, as will be shown farther on. The first example, once again:

Ex.116

The last two eighth-notes before the cadence may create difficulties, but since they occur stepwise they may both be either passed over as unessential, or accompanied with the sixth.

[18] In the third measure of Ex.115b, the first edition gives "3," which the sixth edition emends to "6."

Ex.117

Here is another example, in which the figure begins a third above the key.

Ex.118 (a)

(b)   The same a tone lower

(c)   The same a fifth lower

Another example, beginning a fifth above the key, with a modulation to another key.

Ex.119 [19] (a)

---

[19] The "7" at the beginning of the second measure is, in the first edition, placed over the D in Ex.119a, and omitted in Ex.119b.

(b)   The same a tone higher

Modulation   Return

One may reason, then, from the appearance of the first major semi-tone, that is, the sharp, that the composition is formed on the note a semi-tone above it. For example, if we find G-sharp, it indicates that the composition will be in A; if we find A-sharp, the composition will be in B *mi;* if we find C-sharp, it will be in D—and so on for every key. But in the natural keys F *fa ut* and C *sol fa ut* no accidental major semitones are encountered, and the notes *mi*, that is, E and B, are the semitones. They are natural, and seeing no other accidental it is easy to tell that the composition is formed in one of the two keys, C or F; but the cadences, as I have said, can confirm this. See the examples of these natural keys.

Ex.120   (a)

(b)   At the fifth below

The most necessary and most difficult rule concerns recognizing and foreseeing the modulations and variations of the keys. This, indeed, requires considerable practice, but it can be made easier by remembering always to keep the ear and eye alert for those notes in the progression of the bass that are led up to by a sharp, as mentioned before; continue until a sharp occurs on some other note, whether in the bass itself, or in the signature, or even in the upper part, and deduce from this the key that has been reached. I shall illustrate this with more than one example, but observe carefully that sometimes it is necessary to foresee this accidental two, three, or more notes ahead, and—depending on how it is used —to anticipate it in the accompaniments.

Ex.121

From this example it can be concluded that one accidental cancels another, since, as can be seen, the composition begins in A *la mi re*, where we have at once the accidental G-sharp. Then comes C-sharp (1), which continues as long as no other sharp appears. G-sharp returns (2), canceling the one before. Then comes D-sharp (3), which is the major third of B *mi*, and it, too, cancels the one preceding. D-sharp continues until C-sharp returns (4), which in turn continues until it is canceled by the cadence moving toward C natural (the three notes marked †). Note that without foreseeing this cadence on C, it would have been possible to play a major sixth with E *la mi* because of its relation to the preceding sharp used for the major third of A. But because it must anticipate the following cadence on C, this E takes a minor sixth. The sign, then, of returning to the original key is that same first accidental, the G-sharp, occurring as the major third of E (5), and this sharp follows wherever appropriate until the end of the cadence.

One must not, however, become confused and lose track of the first rules, because what we have given here is a general guide for avoiding bad relationships. For the rest, it is necessary to continue according to the other rules and according to the restrictions imposed by the upper, composed part, for changes in the accidentals may be deceiving, as in the following example.

Ex.122

Here one sees that the added accidentals of a major sixth (at the two notes marked *) do not change the key, but are necessary to a kind of stepwise cadence. But note that the accidental sharp of a sixth cancels the sharp of the third, as seen with the E (at the first *); notice, too, that the major third is canceled by the preceding G natural (marked †). See the rule for descending stepwise in Chapter V.

The minor accidental, the flat, also indicates on occasion a change of key, as in the following.

Ex.123

To provide assurance in the technique of modulating through all the keys, I shall illustrate them all with examples, the mastering of which will give the student great satisfaction.

Ex.124

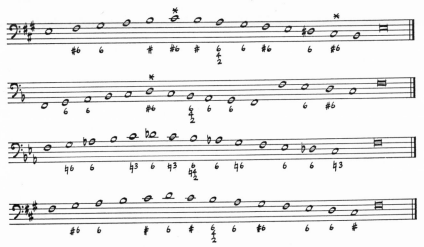

Others of enharmonic or chromatic genus that might occur in the source of modulation

All the keys having a major third must also have a major sixth; those having a minor third must also have a minor sixth. But notice in major keys that the note marked * may have either the major or minor sixth.

In mastering all these examples, be careful not to employ two octaves or two fifths in parallel motion. It is true that two fifths hardly ever succeed each other, since they may be avoided by using sixths, but it is easy to fall into two octaves. But when there is an octave as the highest note in the right hand, move from one note to the next by contrary motion. It is convenient to make use of tenths in the upper part, where they occur naturally. Avoid as much as possible the upper octave of the sharped notes, because then either one falls easily into two octaves, or else the upper part moves awkwardly, creating a bad effect. The doubling of flatted notes in the highest part does no harm, provided one makes use of contrary motion. With these reservations, the filling or doubling of the consonances as much as possible is not a thing to be avoided; nor does one pay such close attention to octaves and fifths in the inner parts, even when they move in parallel motion. This is because they are considered to be evaded by the crossing of the parts, as in compositions for five, six, and eight voices, in which the written parts double the consonances but interchange in such a way that the irregularities forbidden by the valid rules of counterpoint do not occur. I report this opinion from the famous Ruettino [20] of blessed memory, formerly organist of the ducal chapel of St. Mark's in Venice, having seen it in a letter of his written to two musicians. A similar question about the possibility of allowing fifths and octaves in the inner parts of an accompaniment had been raised by these two, and in the letter the question was decisively resolved, in accord with the same reasons I have given here.

I make an exception, however, for accompanying on the organ. Here it is good to make use of the full style in works involving several doubled parts, but in shorter concerted pieces for one or two voices it is much better to use only the essential consonances, without doublings, as if four parts were being played, regarding the act of accompanying as improvised composing. And so, proceeding with the parts sounding together, with the appropriate consonances, with the dissonances and tied notes

[20] Probably Don Giambattista Volpe, called Rovettino (that is, Ruettino), ?–1692?, second organist of St. Mark's in Venice from 11 January 1665, first organist from 9 January 1678, *maestro di cappella* from 6 August 1690.

correctly resolved, as may be appropriate, the composition cannot but go well and to the satisfaction of singer, composer, and listener.

Anyone with the good fortune to have played or studied under the guidance of the renowned Bernardo Pasquini in Rome, or who has at least heard or seen him play, has been privileged to observe the truest, noblest, and most beautiful style of playing and accompanying, and, as a result of his richness of style, has heard from his harpsichord a marvelous perfection of harmony. But let it suffice as an indication of his fame that all the princes of Europe have praised him, in particular His Imperial Majesty Leopold I, who submitted his own musicians to his school and supervision. And I, who had the good fortune to associate with him for a long time, must not, cannot remain silent (permit me to say it): in him was such grace of manner, invariably so well paired with such high virtue, that it might truly be said among our masters:

—Quo justior alter
Nec Virtute fuit, modulis nec major, et arte.

CHAPTER IX

Dissonances in the Recitatives, and How to Play Acciaccaturas

IN RECITATIVES PAY PARTICULAR ATTENTION TO THE COM-
posed part, that is, to the part that is sung. Often above a sustained bass
note the composed part will be dissonant, and after proceeding through
new and different dissonances becomes consonant again, without the
bass having moved. Thus when the composed part begins with a consonance and moves to a second above the bass, harmonize the bass note
by playing simultaneously the second, fourth, and major seventh. Similarly, if the composed part goes to any other of these dissonances, that is
to the fourth or major seventh, do not play one without the others.
Sustain these dissonances until the composed part resolves to a consonance, that is to a third, fifth, or octave. Adding a fifth to these dissonant
notes, next to the fourth, is effective.

78

Ex.125

Sometimes, in these *cantilene* in recitative style, the composed part passes first through a fourth and a sixth, then progresses to a second or major seventh. In such cases play a sixth at the outset, along with the fourth, and nothing else, because it is followed by a progression to the above-mentioned dissonance of a second, fourth, fifth, and major seventh, and this in turn by its resolution, as shown in this example.

Ex.126

The more these dissonances can be played full and doubled, the better will be the effect. Note that when the fourth is augmented, it does not take a seventh, but instead an unprepared second and major sixth.

In order to perform the accompaniments of recitatives with some degree of good taste, the consonances must be deployed almost like an arpeggio, though not continuously so. Once the harmony of a note has been heard, one must hold the keys fast and permit the singer to take the lead, singing at his discretion and in accord with the expression of the words. Do not annoy or disturb him with a continuous arpeggio, or with ascending and descending scale passages, as some do. I do not know whether I should call those performers grandiloquent [*Sonatoroni*] or trivial [*Sonatorelli*] who, in their desire to display their facility, create confusion, and imagine that it is inspiration.

In breaking a full chord as I have described, one can touch fleetingly in the right hand on the semitone just below the upper octave. For example, in harmonizing G *sol re ut* the upper octave is played by the ring finger, and so one strikes the F-sharp with the third finger. Play it with a certain quickness, in the form of a mordent, sounded on, or rather a little before the beat and released immediately, so that it adds a certain grace rather than offending the ear. It is called a mordent [*mordente*, "biting"] because of its resemblance to the bite of a small animal that releases its hold as soon as it bites, and so does no harm. This same mordent may also be played next to the key that forms a third in the right hand—but only in chords of the fifth, and most often when the third is minor. For example, when above the note E *la mi* the index finger of the right hand plays at the octave, the ring finger G, the third, and the little finger B, the fifth, then the mordent falls on the black key F-sharp, which is played by the middle finger. In the following example the numbers above the notes refer to the right hand, those below to the left.

Ex.127

For the sake of clarity, I shall illustrate this as best I can in tablature. Notice that all the notes placed between the barlines are played together at a single stroke.

Ex.128

Generally it may be observed that the mordent is appropriate for the minor third, the octave, and the sixth. But use it judiciously, and not where it creates bad relationships, as for example with the major sixth when combined with a minor third to form a stepwise cadence; for when it falls on the raised fifth the mordent is intolerable, awkward, and pointless.

Ex.129

Sometimes a certain dissonance is used which consists of an *acciaccatura* of two, three, or four notes one close upon the next. This creates an admirable effect, particularly in recitatives or in serious songs, and is found especially with certain notes that take a major sixth, as in the following.

Ex.130

In order to learn this more easily, note that the third and the fourth, sounded together, go well with notes that take a major sixth, and that when possible the seventh is added between sixth and octave; in this way the acciaccatura is formed. It is necessary to employ all the fingers of the right hand and sometimes to play two keys with one finger, usually the thumb. When the diminished fifth is heard over *mi*, or over a note with a sharp, add a minor sixth, and for an acciaccatura a ninth between octave and tenth, creating an excellent effect. The same arrangement serves at the cadences: every time a note calls for both seventh and major third, the fourth, as an acciaccatura, is added between the major third and the fifth.

Ex.131

To those notes calling for a second, an augmented fourth—as already stated, these two do not occur independently—and a major sixth, it is well to add a fifth as an acciaccatura between fourth and sixth.

Ex.132

After this dissonance the mordent to the sixth of the following note (as indicated in the foregoing example) retains its sweetness. One particular passage, found sometimes in recitative and serious arias as well, needs the acciaccatura in order to smooth it over and result in good harmony. This is accomplished as shown here with the vocal part.

Ex.133

The note marked * has an interval the equivalent of a minor third or minor tenth, but which is actually—because of its position—an augmented second or ninth. In playing that note, add a third, an augmented fourth, and above them a sixth, doubling whichever suits you in the left hand. Make use, if you will, of the following example.

Ex.134

The student of harmony must strive to seek out at the keyboard these and similar acciaccaturas in other keys of every genus. After gaining familiarity and ease with them in the natural and diatonic keys, it will be easy to find them in the chromatic or enharmonic keys; but proceed with discretion and with regard for rhythm. Try to find new ones as well—as I did myself when I discovered, in the course of practice, that one can play a certain dissonance (a doubled acciaccatura of fourteen notes) all at one stroke. This occurs, as in the example, when the interval of a major seventh is found in recitative.

Ex.135

In order to play this acciaccatura it is necessary to depress two keys with a single finger at the extremes of both hands, that is, with the little finger and with the thumb. This, however, is an oddity, rather than an example or general rule; its occasional use would be qualified by the considerations of time, place, and company. These and similar dissonances, or harsh harmonies, would seem to allow the good singer scope for better expression of the affections and spirit of compositions. But, as I have said before, use them with discretion, and see to it that you satisfy yourself in the first place, so that in consequence the singer and listener will be better pleased.

You will be able to make equal use of the mordent and acciaccatura in arias or canzonas, since they are essential for playing with grace and good taste; through their use the accompaniment becomes much more harmonious and delightful.

CHAPTER X

Diminution,
Embellishment,
and Adornment
of the Accompaniment

I WOULD LIKE TO SHOW YOU MANY KINDS OF DIMINUTIONS, ornaments, embellishments, and other ways of lending grace to accompaniment. But since these are better expressed in tablature, I shall illustrate only a few of them in certain common passages, so that the student may apply himself with some enjoyment. In these examples the necessary consonances are performed with the left hand, while the right hand plays the upper part as shown below, for instance, in an example of ascending motion by step; other examples [of descending motion by step, of motion by leap and] of certain cadences follow.[21]

[21] In the second measure of the first passage in Ex.136, the fourth note has been changed from a dotted sixteenth. In the second *Cantabile* cadence, a sharp given by the first edition over the penultimate note of the right hand has been read as "tr." At the beginning of the third cadence, also in the right hand, the first edition gives one too many sixteenth-notes.

Ex.136

Descending

With leaps of a third or fourth

Starting from a major third

Common cadences arpeggiated

Cantabile cadences

For approaching a major third

For arriving at an augmented fourth

In this way one may arrive at any sort of accompaniment. I could illustrate many other things, but in order to avoid a pointless excess or confusion, I leave them to the talent, industry, and good taste of the student accompanist, who, as soon as he is capable of playing more than I could put on paper, will, I assume, not have need of such examples, being able to fend for himself by observing attentively the best players and the compositions of the most celebrated composers and masters. One must warn, however, against confusing the singer with such diminu-

tions (or should we say garlands): avoid playing an interval or figure
that he might use. Furthermore, one must never play note for note the
vocal part or other upper composed part for violin, etc., since it suffices
that the harmony contain the consonance or dissonance called for by
the bass and supplied according to the rules of accompaniment.

CHAPTER XI

Diminution or
Adornment of the Bass

I DO NOT APPROVE OF THE DIMINUTION OF THE BASS ITSELF, because it is very easy to miss or depart from the intention of the composer and from the proper spirit of the composition—and to offend the singer. But we say "to accompany" advisedly: he who accompanies must take pride in the title of a good, solid accompanist, not of a spirited and agile performer. He may suit his fancy and unleash his brilliance when he plays alone, not when he accompanies; I, at least, intend to suggest how to play with grace and not with confusion.

Nevertheless, in order that they may be available for the expression of bizarre sentiments, I shall illustrate some diminutions of easy basses. If played with discretion, a steady beat, and a clear idea of the nature of the composition, these diminutions may be used without distorting or altering the intention of the composer. I shall give several examples, the first moving in quarter-notes.

Ex.137 (a)

(b)

Seeing that this is an arpeggio drawn from the consonances themselves, it will be easy for the student to learn—but it should be used with discretion.

Ex.138

Another way

Another way in a faster tempo

In triple, or some other proportion

Another way

If the tempo is faster

In certain eighth-note patterns

Another way

In using these and similar diminutions, all the required consonances should be played in the right hand. As to their use, I completely approve it in ritornellos and when the singer is silent; beyond this, I refer the matter to the prudence and discretion of the accompanist, who must decide what is appropriate. Actually (to speak more directly), if I had not known the world to be full of people of various inclinations and different dispositions, I would neither have expounded nor approved of diminution, in the knowledge that the wisest men will call the examples that I have given trifles or childish tricks. I cannot condemn the opinions of such men; but whoever wishes to use diminution—and can do so wisely and at the right moment—can ignore these opinions. I, for my part, declare my motive to have been the introduction of some sort of relief and delight to the labors of present-day students of harmony.

From the examples above you will also understand that when certain basses using diminution and containing leaps are found in compositions for the theatre or the chamber, these are in fact in the form of arpeggios; therefore the notes between the counts must be passed over and not accompanied. This may be observed at the opening of my *Cantate da Camera* printed as Opus I [22] at the words "A battaglia o miei pensieri"; the bass goes like this:

Ex.139

Notice carefully that the underlying pattern of these notes is this:

Ex.140

[22] *Cantate da Camera a voce sola . . . Opera prima*, Rome, Mascardi, 1695.

Many such motifs, of various kinds, may be observed in the cantatas of many excellent composers—but especially in those cantatas by Giovanni Bononcini, most worthy Virtuoso of His Imperial Majesty. In these cantatas you will discern no little *bizzaria*, beauty, harmony, artful study, and fanciful invention, because of which they justly receive the applause of the whole world in admiration of his most delightful talent.

It seems to me that I have finally presented and illustrated enough; it is the extent of what I know and can expound about the rules, observations, and styles of good accompaniment. There remains only to illustrate how to transpose, in order that this may be done with ease.

CHAPTER XII

How to Transpose through All Keys

I CONSIDER TRANSPOSITION THROUGH EVERY KEY AND GENUS essential to the good organist. But since this comes exclusively with practice, I can think of no better way than to make a special point of knowing all the clefs instinctively; thus when it becomes necessary to transpose a fourth, fifth, or third, either up or down, or a second higher or lower, one can picture immediately in which clef to read the composition. In order to be able to do this easily, study carefully the following table and notice how the clefs are placed for any sort of transposition.

Ex.141

Without accidentals

A tone higher:
Mezzo-soprano clef on the second line

A third higher:
Baritone clef on the third line

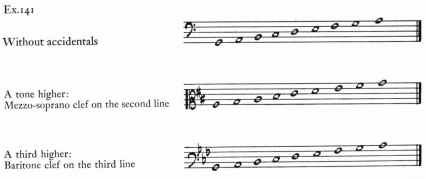

A fourth higher, or a fifth lower:
Soprano clef on the first line

A fifth higher, or a fourth lower:
Tenor clef on the fourth line

A tone lower:
Contralto clef on the third line

A minor third lower:
Violin clef on the second line,
Or bass clef on the fifth line

A major third lower:
The same

A semitone higher:
Mezzo-soprano clef on the second line

With flats

A tone higher

A third higher

A fourth higher

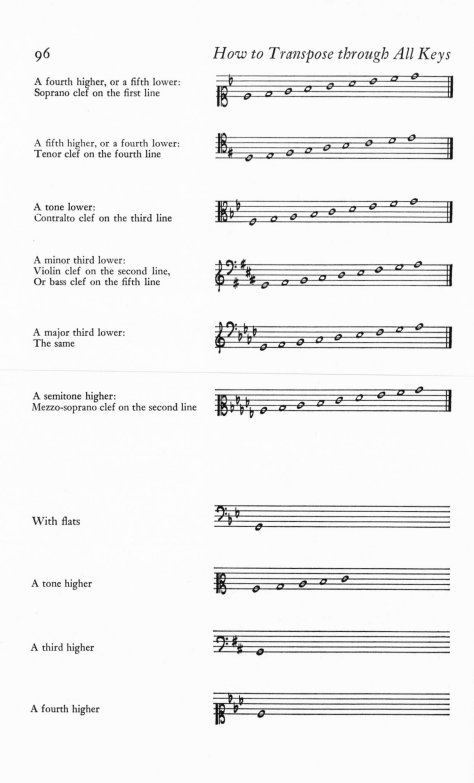

A fifth higher

A tone lower

A third lower

A semitone higher

A semitone lower

One must note which transpositions of keys with sharps or flats are least inconvenient and most natural.

Ex.142

[With sharps]

A tone higher is possible, using this clef

A semitone higher is more convenient, using this clef

A third higher is perfectly easy

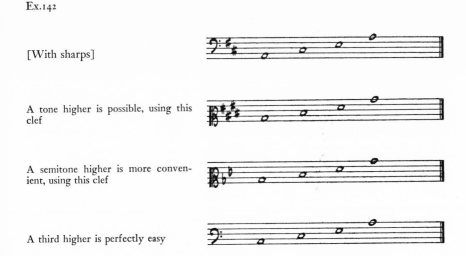

A fourth higher, or a fifth lower

A fifth higher, or a fourth lower

A tone lower

A third lower

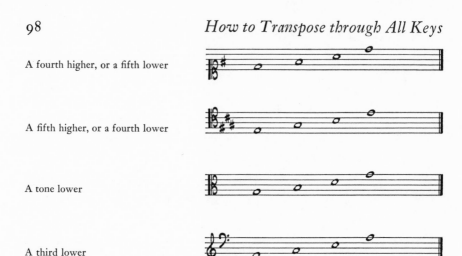

It is necessary to play the clefs of the acute and superacute registers an octave lower so that the accompaniment is proper and conforms to what is required by the nature of the bass or foundation.

The key of B-flat (see the next example) may be transposed a semitone higher if so desired, but it is a little inconvenient because of the many sharps; still, it is easy to read because the bass clef is retained, it being necessary only to imagine the sharps added to it.

Ex.143

[Key of B-flat]

[A semitone higher]

A semitone lower is convenient, using this clef

A tone higher is perfectly easy, using this clef

A third higher, using this clef

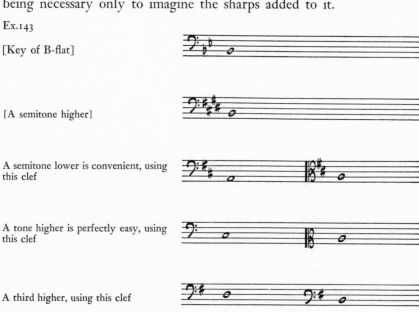

A third lower, using this clef

A fourth higher, or a fifth lower, using this clef

A fifth higher, or a fourth lower, using this clef

From these examples one can generally tell which clef to use for any transposition. In order to be more secure in their use, one can memorize the following rules.

A tone higher becomes mezzo-soprano (C-clef on the second line).

A third higher becomes baritone (C-clef on the third line).

A fourth higher,

    or a fifth lower, becomes soprano (C-clef on the first line).

A fifth higher,

    or a fourth lower, becomes tenor (C-clef on the fourth line).

A tone lower becomes contralto (C-clef on the third line).

A third lower becomes violin G *sol re ut* (on the second line).

One must next determine of which type the composition is, whether that with a major third or with a minor third, either natural or altered, then make appropriate use of the correct accidentals; otherwise great disorder could arise, changing the quality of the key, and the composition would be ruined. For this reason be sure to retain the same species of fourth and fifth, so that they remain correct, and make use of accidentals where necessary in order to reproduce each interval as it occurs in the composition. I could illustrate other ways of transposing, but I regard this as superfluous, for when the student is capable of using the examples already given he can investigate all the other keys by himself, and with study will become skilled and efficient in every sort of transposition. In order easily to gain a full knowledge of the clefs, study the following table, proceeding from the grave to the most acute register.

Ex.144   *Table of all the musical clefs*

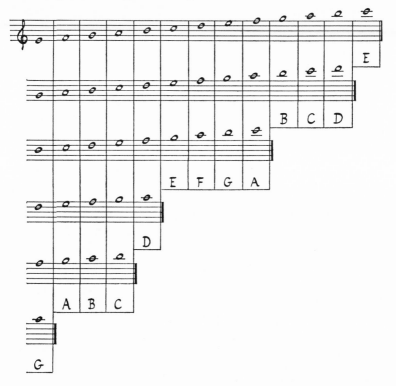

Any transposition becomes very easy if this exercise in all the clefs is clearly understood. And this is as much as I can describe and set forth to aid and satisfy you; your perceptive talent will make up for my imperfections. In any case, rest content and judge me leniently. If I have not supported my reasoning by citing the authority of the masters, either of classical antiquity or of modern times, in order to convince you that my teachings are approved, you must recall that I have neither discoursed on counterpoint nor treated the art of harmony in general. This material has been sufficiently dealt with in the excellent study of Zarlino, and by many other celebrated authors, and finally so ably expressed by the Very Reverend Father Baccelliere Zaccaria Tevo, of the Friars Minor Conventual in his *Musico Testore* [Bortoli, 1706]. I have shown you but a manner of accompaniment—how to realize a bass at a keyboard instrument; in all matters I have endeavored to rely on the valid rules of counterpoint. If you derive some profit from my work, do not attribute it to my glory, of which I am not desirous; but rather to the glory of the Most High, who gave me the inspiration for it. If my work seems useless or inaccurate to you, accept only the good will behind it. If you are pleased with it, do not fail to avail yourself of it, since it is my hope that it will aid you; and if it does not suffice to sustain and satisfy you, rest assured that after learning this much *Usus te plura docebit.*

THE END